DISCOVERING
METALS

Carmel Reilly

Rigby

www.Rigby.com
1-800-531-5015

Rigby Focus Forward

Published in 2007 by Nelson Australia Pty Ltd ACN: 058 280 149
A Cengage Learning company

1 2 3 4 5 6 7 8 374 14 13 12 11 10 09 08 07
Printed and bound in China

Discovering Metals
ISBN-13   978-1-4190-3837-2
ISBN-10   1-4190-3837-0

Acknowledgments
The author and publisher would like to acknowledge permission to reproduce material
from the following sources:
Photographs by AAA Collection/ Ronald Sheridan, p. 21 right; AKG Images, front cover
bottom, pp. 1 bottom, 19 right/ Erich Lessing, pp. 4, 20; Corbis/ Angelo Hornak, p. 8
bottom/ Jonathan Blair, p. 16; Fotolia/ Elvira Schäfer, p. 6 left/ Steffen Foerster, p. 6 right/
Thomas Brostrom, p. 23 bottom right; Getty Images/ Aurora, p.5/ Hulton Archives,
p.11/ National Geographic, p. 17; Masterfile/ Peter Griffith, p. 23 left; PhotoDisc, front
cover (background), p. 13; Photolibrary/ Dinodia, front cover top, pp. 1 top, 10 left/
Joyce Productions, p. 9 left/ JTB Photo, p. 9 right/ Photo Researchers, p. 12/ Sinclair
Stammers, p. 18/ SPL/ Kaj Svensson, p. 8 top/ The Bridgeman Art Library, back cover, pp.
7 left, 7 right, 14 top, 22; The Art Archive/ Historiska Museet Stockholm/ Dagli Orti, p.
21 left/ Ironbridge Gorge Museum, p. 23 top right/ Musee Cernuschi Paris/ Dagli Orti,
p. 14 bottom/ Museo Civico Udine/ Dagli Orti (A), p. 15 left/ Museo Nazionale d'Arte
Orientale Rome / Dagli Orti, p. 10 right/ Prehistoric Museum Moesgard Hojbjerg
Denmark/ Dagli Orti, pp. 3, 15 right, 19 left.

DISCOVERING METALS

Carmel Reilly

Contents

Chapter 1

THE END OF THE STONE AGE

The Stone Age is the name given to an early period in history when people made their tools and weapons out of stone.

The Stone Age started more than one million years ago. It finished when people began to replace their stone tools and weapons with those made out of metal.

a weapon made of copper and bone

The Stone Age didn't end at the same time
around the world.
For example, in places like the Middle East,
it ended about 6,000 years ago
when people there started using copper.

people in Papua New Guinea

In other places, like Papua New Guinea,
the Stone Age ended only quite recently
because the people of that country
didn't discover metal (or know how to use it)
until they had contact with Westerners.

Chapter 2

DISCOVERING METALS

Gold

Gold was probably the first metal
to be discovered by humans.
It is believed that gold was first used
about 8,000 years ago.

Gold was ideal for making jewelry and ornaments because it is a soft metal.
It would later become important in trade and for making coins.
However, gold wasn't strong enough to make tools or weapons.
Therefore it didn't have a big effect on the lives of Stone Age people.

Copper

Copper was discovered about 6,000 years ago.
It had a much bigger impact on Stone Age people's
lives than gold had.
Although copper is now commonly used to make
pots and pans, during the Stone Age
people needed copper to make tools and weapons.

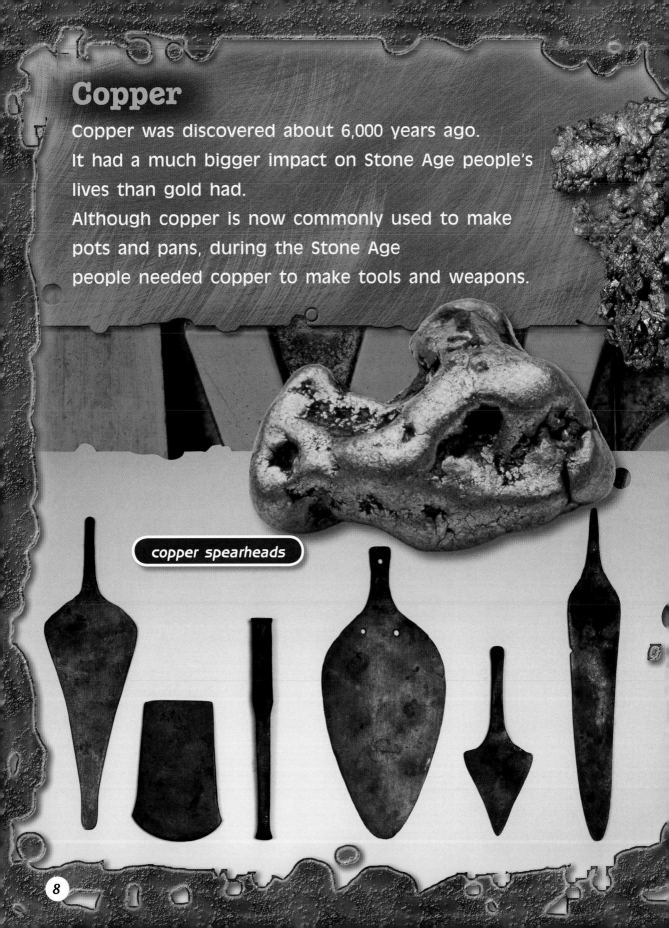

copper spearheads

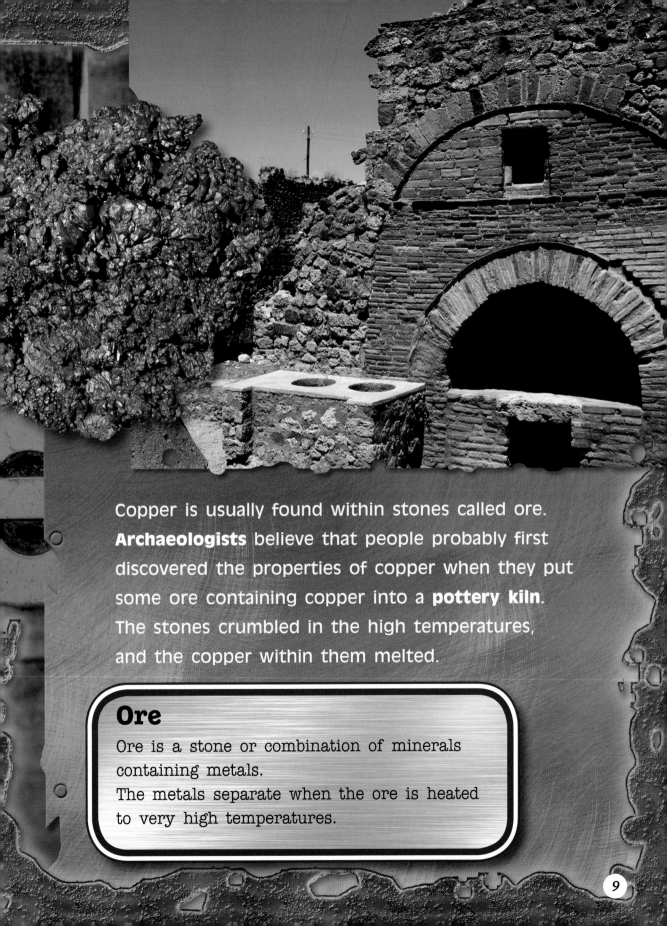

Copper is usually found within stones called ore.
Archaeologists believe that people probably first
discovered the properties of copper when they put
some ore containing copper into a **pottery kiln**.
The stones crumbled in the high temperatures,
and the copper within them melted.

Ore

Ore is a stone or combination of minerals
containing metals.
The metals separate when the ore is heated
to very high temperatures.

Chapter 3

WORKING METALS

People observed that as melted copper cooled, it became hard.

Soon they realized that being able to melt this metal meant they could shape it and make it into ornaments, tools, and utensils.

These people became the first metal workers.

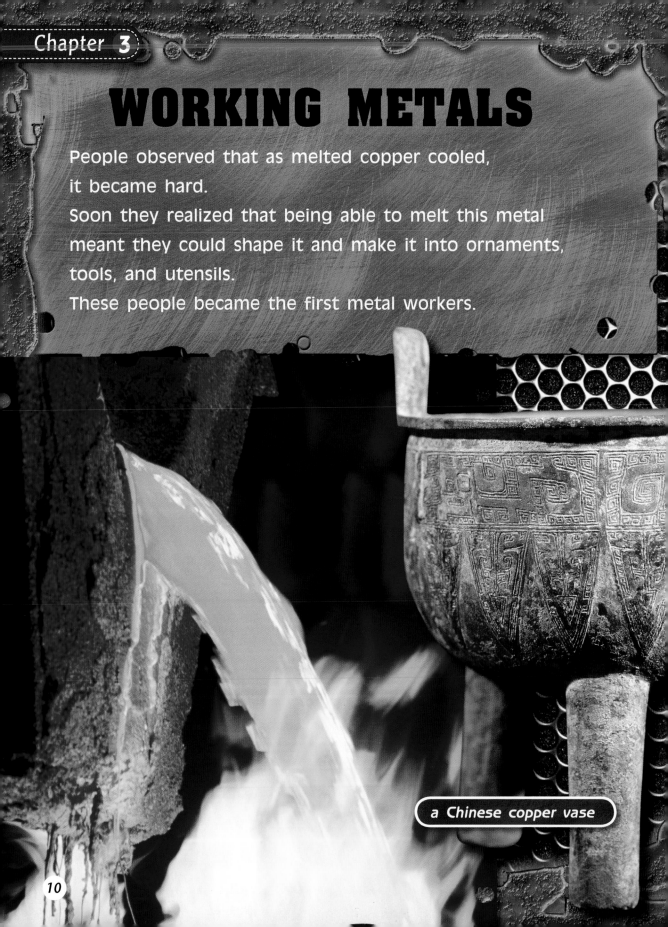

a Chinese copper vase

Metal workers worked out how to smelt metal—
that is, how to melt ore in order to produce
metal from it.

Later they worked out how to make molds
for the metal so that they could create
the exact shapes they wanted.

Chapter 4

BRONZE

In places such as China, the Middle East, and parts of Europe, another metal—tin—was found near copper.

tin

Metal workers in these places discovered that if tin and copper were mixed together, they became much harder when they set. This new metal was called bronze.

bronze

Alloy

An alloy is a mixture of two or more metals. Metals can be mixed together to give them special properties, such as strength, lightness, or flexibility.

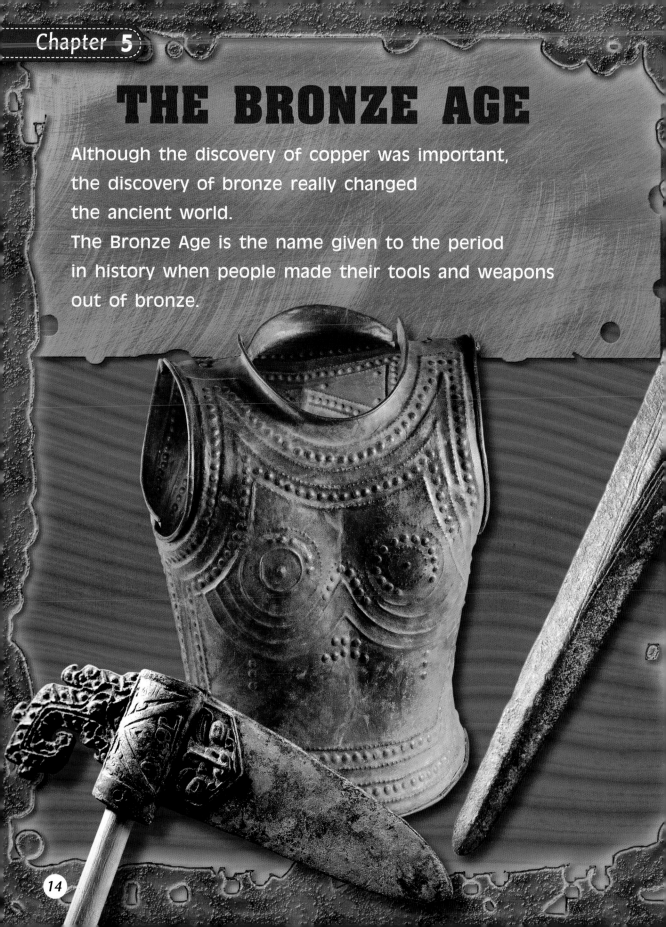

Chapter 5

THE BRONZE AGE

Although the discovery of copper was important,
the discovery of bronze really changed
the ancient world.
The Bronze Age is the name given to the period
in history when people made their tools and weapons
out of bronze.

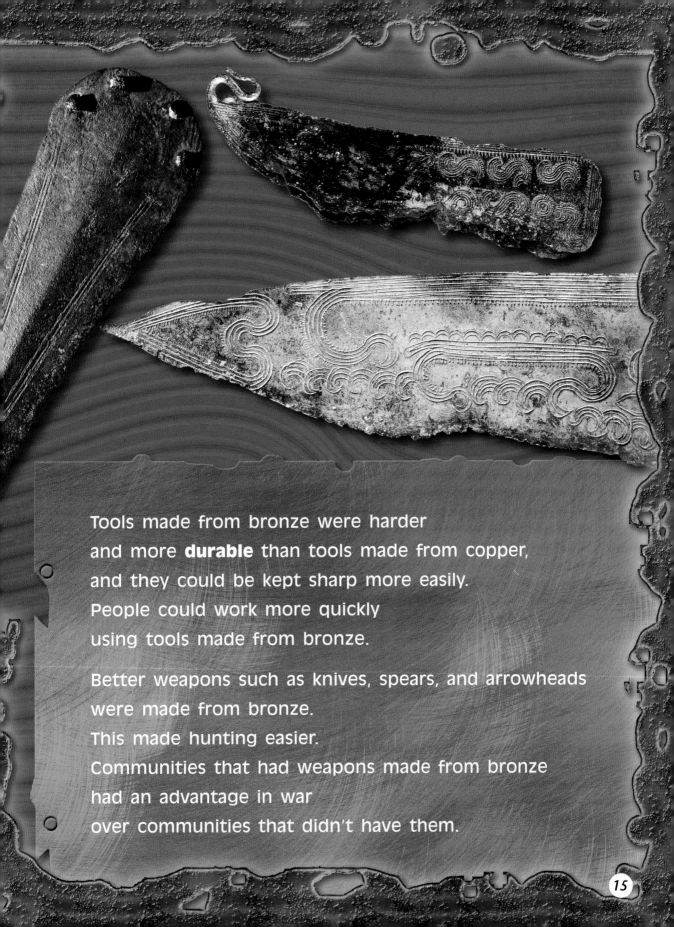

Tools made from bronze were harder
and more **durable** than tools made from copper,
and they could be kept sharp more easily.
People could work more quickly
using tools made from bronze.

Better weapons such as knives, spears, and arrowheads
were made from bronze.
This made hunting easier.
Communities that had weapons made from bronze
had an advantage in war
over communities that didn't have them.

A Prized Product

Bronze became a prized product
because of its many uses.
Those communities with good access
to copper and tin
specialized in bronze metalwork.
Archaeologists have found metalworking sites,
dating back more than 5,000 years,
in Turkey, the south of Spain,
and in the **Balkans.**

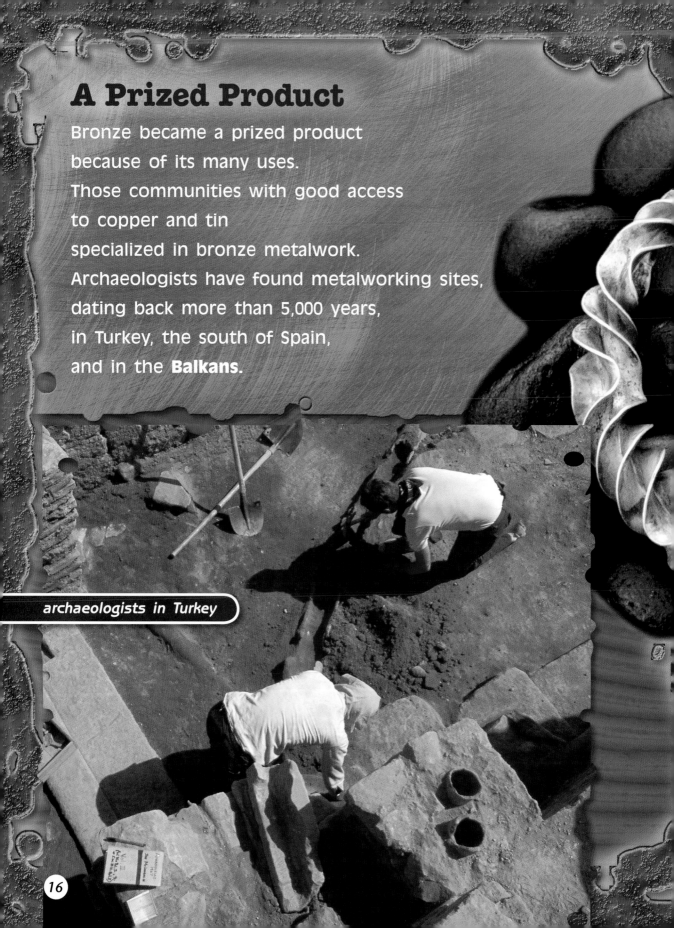

archaeologists in Turkey

Around this time, people started trading
in bronze.
Some communities imported bronze goods,
while other communities imported copper and tin ore
to smelt and turn into bronze themselves.

Chapter 6

THE IRON AGE

Iron was first used about 3,500 years ago.
The Iron Age is the name given to the period
in history when people made
their tools and weapons out of iron.

Although iron ore was common,
people took longer to discover its uses
because it was harder to smelt than gold,
copper, and tin.
The temperature for melting iron was much higher
than for these metals, and special conditions were needed
to melt iron.

iron ore

Melting Points of Metals

Tin	449.6°F
Gold	1,943.6°F
Copper	1,983.2°F
Iron	2,795°F

Viking swords made from iron

a seventh century iron helmet

Better than Bronze

Two things about iron made it more useful than bronze.
First iron was much harder than bronze.
Second it was more plentiful than bronze, and over time, it became cheaper to use.

Because iron was plentiful and cheap, Iron Age communities were able to make more tools and weapons.
Over time people made larger tools, such as **plows**, which made working the land easier.

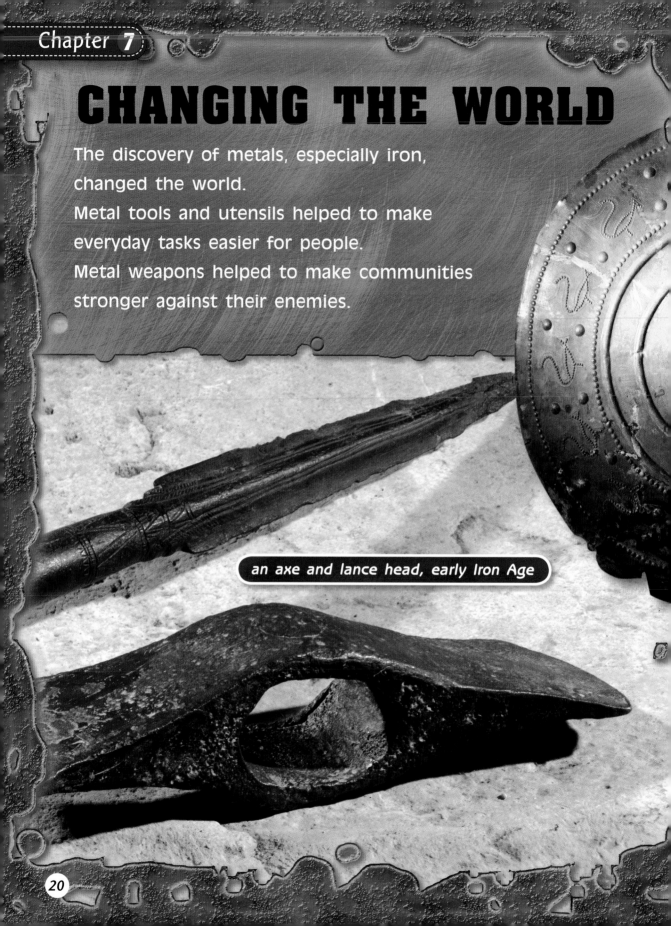

Chapter 7

CHANGING THE WORLD

The discovery of metals, especially iron, changed the world.
Metal tools and utensils helped to make everyday tasks easier for people.
Metal weapons helped to make communities stronger against their enemies.

an axe and lance head, early Iron Age

a bronze shield, Bronze Age

electrum coins from Lydia, 600 B.C.

About 4,000 years ago, metal coins were developed.
People realized that coins were a good way
of exchanging goods and paying people
for work they had done.
The use of coins also helped the development
of trade and communication
between different communities.

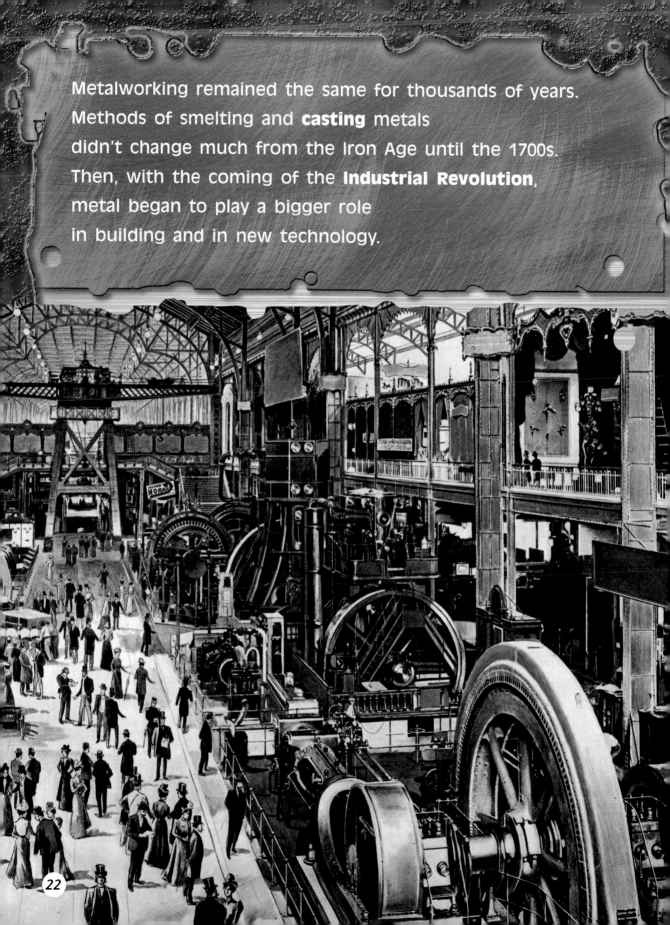

Metalworking remained the same for thousands of years. Methods of smelting and **casting** metals didn't change much from the Iron Age until the 1700s. Then, with the coming of the **Industrial Revolution**, metal began to play a bigger role in building and in new technology.

Casting large pieces of iron and steel
led to the development of large buildings and bridges.
Trains were cast from iron,
and engines were made from iron and other metal alloys.
Since the 1700s, many new kinds of metals
have been discovered,
and the smelting and processing of metals
has been refined.
Today metals are an important and essential part
of most people's lives.

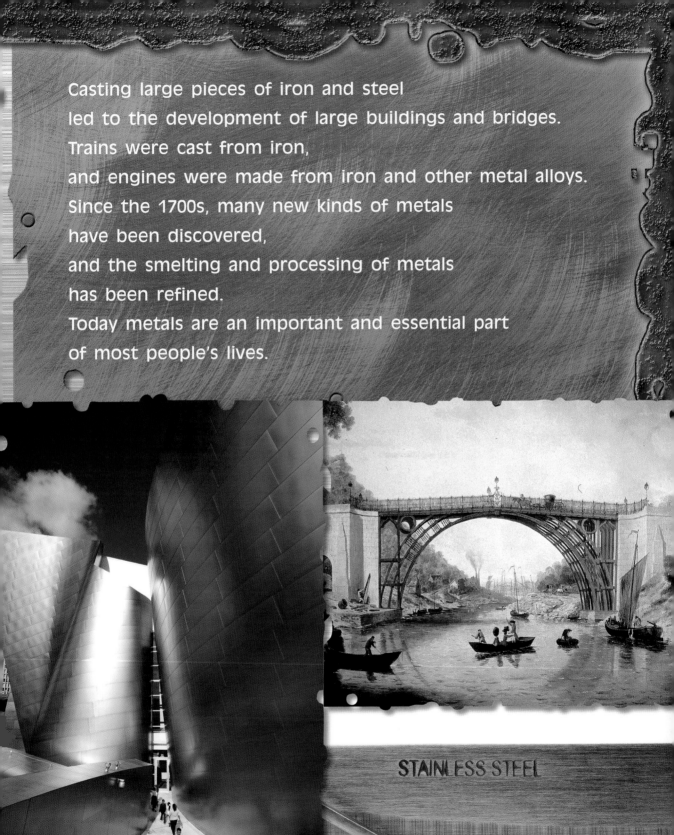

STAINLESS STEEL

Glossary

archaeologists   people who study human history through the recovery and analysis of remains and environmental data

Balkans   the group of countries occupying the area of south-eastern Europe

casting   shaping metals by pouring them into a mold

durable   hard-wearing

Industrial Revolution   a time (late eigthteenth and early nineteenth centuries) when machinery and industry replaced the use of manual labor

plows   tools used in farming for the cultivation of soil in preparation for planting crops. Plows were pulled by humans, oxen, or horses.

pottery kiln   a chamber, like an oven, used to fire and harden clay

Index